May these wonderful words and special insights provide you with encouragement and joy…

and may they help to inspire your life!

ISBN: 978-1-68088-424-1 (previously ISBN: 978-1-59842-906-0)

Printed in China.
First printing of this edition: 2023

This book is printed on recycled paper.

This book is printed on paper that has been specially produced to be acid free (neutral pH) and contains no groundwood or unbleached pulp. It conforms with the requirements of the American National Standards Institute, Inc., so as to ensure that this book will last and be enjoyed by future generations.

Blue Mountain Arts, Inc.
P.O. Box 4549, Boulder, Colorado 80306

Make Every Day a Positive One

A book of encouragement, hope, and great advice

Douglas Pagels

Blue Mountain Press™
Boulder, Colorado

I have some good news about your future.

Yesterday is behind you. What's done is done, and it's important for you to take what you've learned from the past and just move on. Today is a brand-new opportunity, a blank canvas, an unwritten page... just waiting for you. All that needs to happen right now is for you to do all the amazing things you're capable of...

And tomorrow? That's the place where promises come true. You'll need to be smart and stay strong to live the life you want to have. But don't ever forget: you are creative and capable and wise, and I know you have what it takes to make your days everything you want them to be. And remember this for sure…

You can't change a single thing about the past, but you can change absolutely everything about the future.

When you are wonderfully on
the way to becoming all that you
were meant to be...

the happiness you feel inside
is your life smiling.

May the days be so good to you

May they be giving more often than taking. And comforting more often than crazy. May the passing seasons make sure that any heartaches are replaced with a million smiles and that any hard journeys eventually turn into nice, easy miles that take you everywhere you want to go. May your memories become ones you'll always treasure, and may so many moments bring smiles to your eyes.

And may you always believe in happy endings, because you are the author of the story of your life.

Always make time for you

Sometimes it's important to work for that pot of gold. But other times it's essential to take time off and to make sure that your most important decision in the day simply consists of choosing which color to slide down on the rainbow.

And it's good to remember every day that... the secret joys of living are not found by rushing from point A to point B, but by slowing down and inventing some imaginary letters along the way.

When your heart is filled with gratitude
for what you do have…

your head isn't nearly so worried
about what you don't.

May you be blessed with all these things

A little more joy, a little less stress, a lot more recognition of your wonderfulness.

Abundance in your life, blessings in your days, dreams that come true, and hopes that stay.

A rainbow on the horizon, an angel by your side, and everything that could ever bring a smile to your life.

Don't ever forget how special you really are

As you go through life, try to remember these gentle words of reassurance…

"I know there will be days when I may be less than some people prefer me to be, but most people are unaware that I am so much more than what they see."

Be authentic.
Genuine. Honest. Sincere. Flaws and all. Assets galore. Don't pretend to be someone else. Just be you. One-of-a-kind, remarkable, refreshing, what-a-blessing-to-have-you-here… you!

As you journey along through life, remember these words every day: You were given the gift of being simply amazing. And no one can ever take that away.

Don't be passive when you need to be active. Don't just imagine yourself living more fully. If you want to change and be a better you, it's time to turn off any old excuses and embrace new possibilities. Do what will make the "future you" so happy about the love you've decided to show yourself and the wonderful plans you've put in place. Be a person who makes a point of living more fully and who – when waking up in the morning – has a lot more smiles to greet the day.

Sometimes it's a beautiful day just because it is. And sometimes it's a beautiful day because you were creative and brave and you followed your bliss.

Journey one day at a time

Today...

How precious it is, and how full of possibilities. How sad it would be to waste it worrying about the future, and how wrong it would be to spend it dwelling on problems from the past.

Today... is here. Today is now. Today is filled with as much magic as you want to give it. Today is filled with amazing grace waiting for you to live it.

Whenever you get to a turning point in your life, think of it as a chance to turn into more of the person you want to be.

One great decision made at one special time in your life can lead to everything after being better and shining brighter.

Your belief in yourself
and the best in you...
can rise above anything that life
tries to put you through.

Always have something to
look forward to.

Set an intention.
What do you want to accomplish in the weeks, months, and years ahead? Write your intention down and tape it to a mirror where you'll see it every day. Use it as a loving reminder of where you're headed and why you're going in that direction.

And then, when you see the reflection of a wonderful person smiling back at you, you'll also see who you're making happy as the goal gets closer and closer to being met.

Making that positive change

Here's a goal for the day:

I'm going to take things one step at a time.
I will realize the worth of this moment
and the wonder of a new beginning.
I will remember what a treasure
I am holding in my hands, and I will say
a quiet thanks for the opportunity and
the promise… of this brand-new day.

Here's a motto for the week:

I will turn to the courage within me.
I will add richness to my life.
I will go without the things that should be left behind, knowing that once those anchors are no longer holding me down, my spirit can lift me up so much easier...
and I can rise above anything.
I can dream my dreams. I can do so much.
I can be someone I'm so proud of.

And here's a message for the month:

I will take all those positive steps, all those promises, and all those opportunities... and put them together into one great result. My heart will be so much fuller than it was just a month ago. My dreams will be a lot closer than they were only a few weeks ago. My confidence will just shine, because I will have spent the last thirty days polishing it up. I'll be looking at things from a brand-new point of view. My progress will be obvious to everyone. But especially... to me.

And when I look in the mirror,
nothing's going to be sweeter
than smiling right back...
at the wonderful person I see.

You've got this

You have so much going for you. You have gifts that have never even been opened and personal journeys waiting to be explored. You are a special person and you have a future that is in the best of hands.

And you need to remember: if you have plans you want to act on and dreams you've always wanted to come true…

You have what it takes, because…
you have you.

There's so much wisdom to be found in the old adage that says, "You can't always have a good day. But you can always face a bad day with a good attitude."

I think that keeping a positive attitude helps immensely when you're in the process of seeing your way through. Life will always have its ups and downs, but don't ever forget: you are a remarkable person who can hang tough, hold on, and balance things out. Rely on your smile, reflect on your faith, go one step at a time, and just stay strong.

Having the right attitude helps us spend less time in the whirlwind of life… and more time in the calm.

Some assembly is required

Most of us have a put-together life, rather than one that has effortlessly blossomed into what it is today.

Every new day brings us changes and gives us chances... to revise and rebuild, take away from, add to, and make our life take the kind of shape we want it to.

When we're putting our lives together, let's try to have them consist of these things...

A loving, comforting sense of ourselves. An appreciation for how completely unique we are. Refreshing amounts of optimism. The sweet blessings of true friendship and reciprocal love. Laughter. Caring and kindness. Understanding and grace. And the wisdom to always listen...

to what our hearts are trying to say.

You are personally responsible
for so much of the sunshine
that brightens up your life.

Positive people and gentle souls
continually benefit from their
very own versions of daylight
saving time. They get extra hours
of happiness and sunshine
...every day.

If you happen to be reading this and it isn't already a wonderful day, smile and think about it. Chances are... there's still something you can do to make it that way.

Many of the moments ahead will be marvelously disguised as ordinary days.

But each one of us has the chance to make something extraordinary out of them.

Go through the days ahead with
greater self-acceptance and a goal of
finding a way to bring everything in
your life into balance.

Let the roots of all your dreams go deep.
Let the hopes of all your tomorrows
grow high.
Bend, but don't break.
Take the seasons as they come.
Stick up for yourself.

And reach for the sky.

Find a nice sheet of paper
and your very best pen.
Then... get lost in your thoughts and
write out your definition of success.

Fill it with a mix of stardust and wishes
and down-to-earth things, and provide
all the insight you can give it.

Imagine what it takes to have a happy life.

And then go out... and live it.

May you be blessed with... being in a place where there are a thousand more smiles than frowns. Where there are hugs and love and dear, sweet friends. A place where life is the good kind of crazy – and there's so much to be proud of. Where the things that matter most, matter most. I pray that the days will always take you there.

That's where the magic happens.

You deserve all the happiness in the world. And I hope that's exactly what you're blessed with.

Do all those special things that help your heart remember what a gift each day can be. Have fun. Be brave. Make a difference. And have faith. Realize that people are the treasures in life, and happiness is the real wealth.

Stay positive every day and keep doing your best... and the rest will take care of itself.

About the Author

Best-selling author and editor Douglas Pagels has inspired millions of readers with his insights and anthologies. His books have sold over 3.5 million copies, and he is one of the most quoted contemporary writers on social media and online today.

His writings have been translated into over a dozen languages due to their global appeal and inspiring outlook on life, and his audience has now increased even more — thanks to his very popular line of pix & pagels greeting cards, books, calendars, and gift items. Visit www.douglaspagels.com to find out more about the author and this wonderful, colorful, and one-of-a-kind collection.

Be sure to keep this book close in the months and years to come. It will always be good to visit again, and it will bring you smiles and warm your heart every time you do.